The Little Book of
GOOD MANNERS

By Zack Bush and Laurie Friedman
Illustrated by Sarah Van Evera

THIS BOOK BELONGS TO:

_____

WHAT are they?

WHO needs them?

HOW DO YOU GET THEM?

WHY ARE THEY IMPORTANT?

For answers to these questions, just turn the page!

GOOD MANNERS are when you use your words, actions, and deeds to show other people that you care about them.

When you use **GOOD MANNERS,** you not
only make others feel good. You will feel good too.

A great way to show your GOOD MANNERS
is by carefully choosing your words.

Polite, kind words are like magic. When you use them,
people will instantly feel good and smile.

What are some of the best words to choose?

Saying **PLEASE** when you want
something shows thoughtfulness for others.

Saying **THANK YOU** when someone does something nice for you demonstrates appreciation and gratitude. You can even write a **THANK-YOU** note.

Another polite thing to say is **EXCUSE ME.** Say it if . . .

You bump into someone.

Interrupt them.

Want their attention.

Get attention
you don't want!

Some of the most important words that display **GOOD MANNERS** are **I'M SORRY**.

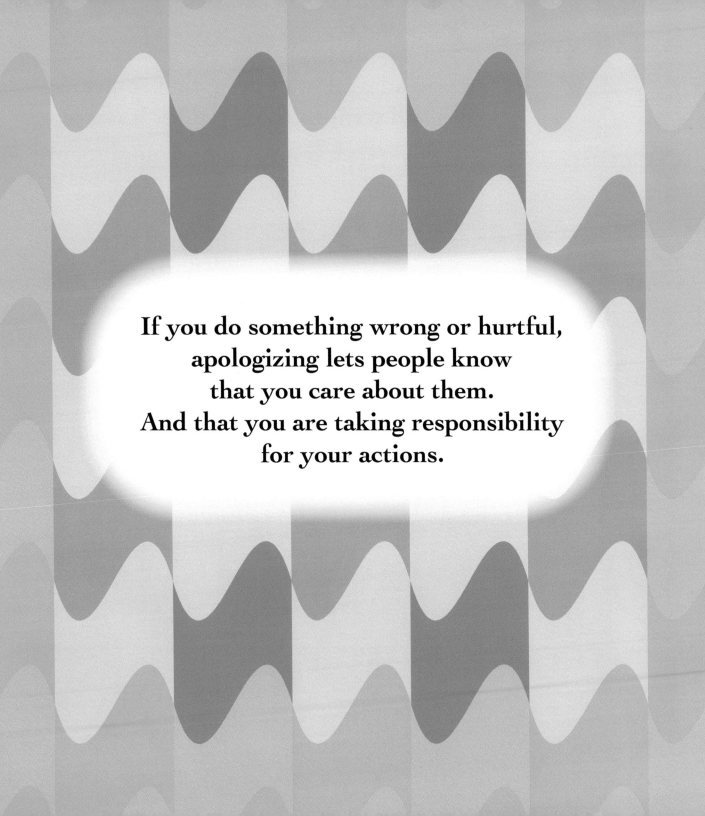

If you do something wrong or hurtful,
apologizing lets people know
that you care about them.
And that you are taking responsibility
for your actions.

When you admire something that someone did and want to show praise, it is **GOOD MANNERS** to give a compliment.

GOOD JOB!

WELL DONE:

I'M PROUD!

Awesome!

THAT MAKES ME SMILE!

Way to go!

You're amazing!

YOUR HARD
WORK SHOWS!

Sometimes the best way to show your **GOOD MANNERS** is to say nothing.

A good time to practice being quiet is in the classroom. Don't interrupt when your teacher is talking. Listen quietly and follow directions. If you have a question, raise your hand.

1 2

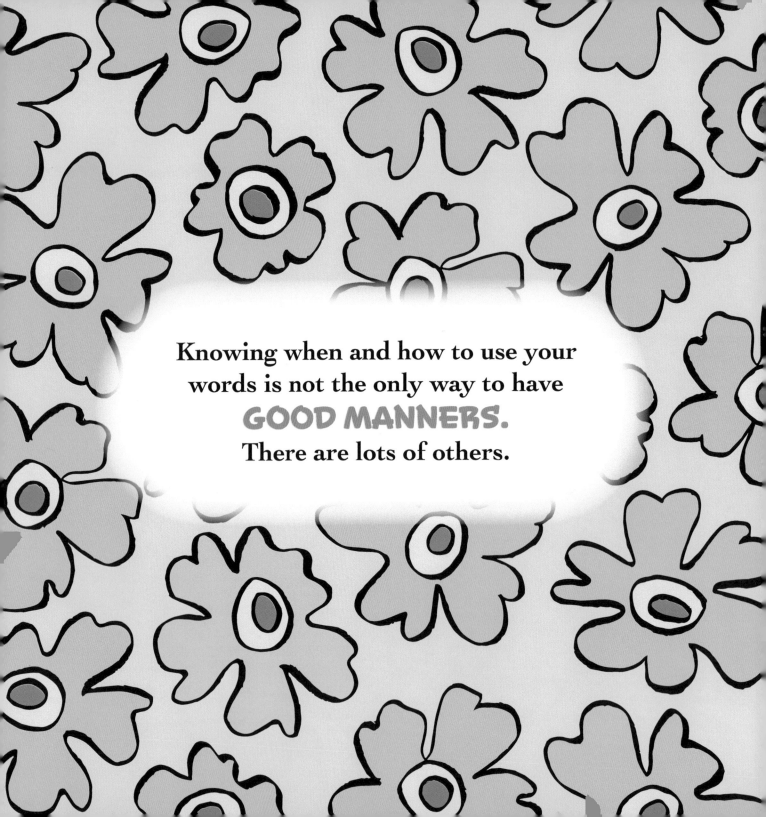

Knowing when and how to use your words is not the only way to have **GOOD MANNERS.** There are lots of others.

POOL RULES

No running
Wait your turn
Pick up trash
Swim with a buddy

Following rules is a great way to show your **GOOD MANNERS.** There are lots of places where you can practice following the rules. At home. On the playground. In the library. At the pool.

Cleaning up after yourself is another way to show that you have **GOOD MANNERS.**

And when you're done playing, if you put things back where they belong, they won't get lost or broken.

It's also really **GOOD MANNERS**
to clean up after your pet!

There are other ways to show that you know what it means to have **GOOD MANNERS.**

Wait for your turn.

Knock before entering.

Offer to help.

Practice sharing.

Cover your mouth.

And wash
your hands.

One place to use your **GOOD MANNERS** is at your table at home.

-SIT UP STRAIGHT

-PUT YOUR NAPKIN IN YOUR LAP

-CLEAR YOUR PLATE WHEN DONE

-LEARN TO HOLD YOUR

KNIFE AND FORK

And remember to use your **GOOD MANNERS**
when you eat out at a restaurant.

When is the best time to use your
MANNERS?

Any time . . . day or night is a good
time to be thoughtful and polite.

Not sure what to do to show that you have
GOOD MANNERS?
Here's a simple trick: just smile!

Sometimes smiling can make you feel better.
And it will make other people feel good too.

Learning to have **GOOD MANNERS** takes time and practice.

When you use **GOOD MANNERS,** people will notice.
They will see and appreciate that you are
making an effort to be polite and thoughtful.

And remember . . . the best way to show that you have **GOOD MANNERS** is to treat people how you want to be treated.

CONGRATULATIONS!

Here's your GOOD MANNERS badge.

Just print it out and pin it on.

Go to the website
www.BooksByZackAndLaurie.com
to print out your badge from
the Printables & Activities page.

And if you like this book, please go to
Amazon and leave a kind review.

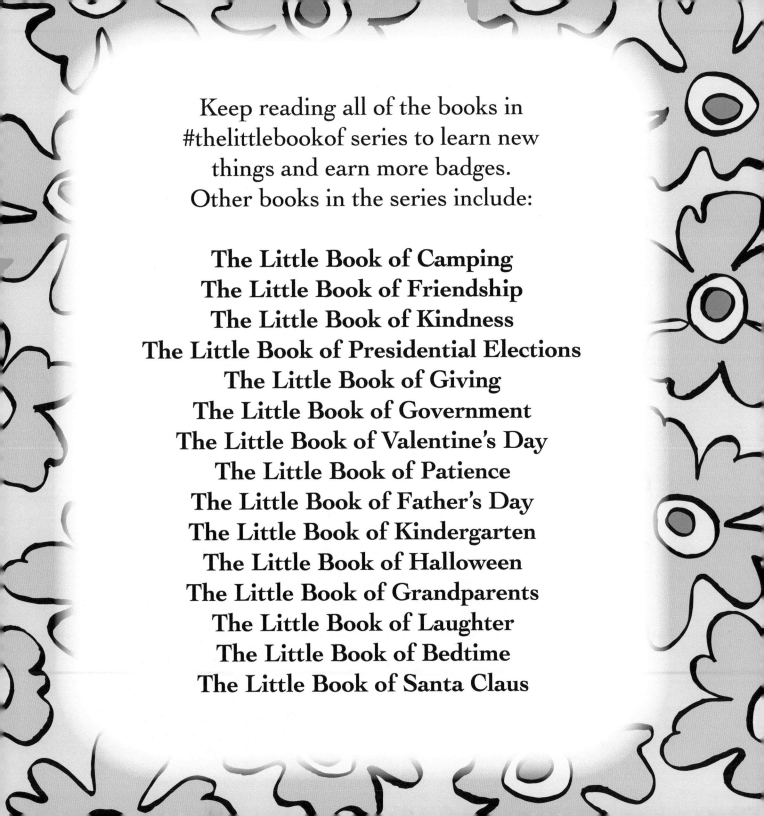

Keep reading all of the books in
#thelittlebookof series to learn new
things and earn more badges.
Other books in the series include:

The Little Book of Camping
The Little Book of Friendship
The Little Book of Kindness
The Little Book of Presidential Elections
The Little Book of Giving
The Little Book of Government
The Little Book of Valentine's Day
The Little Book of Patience
The Little Book of Father's Day
The Little Book of Kindergarten
The Little Book of Halloween
The Little Book of Grandparents
The Little Book of Laughter
The Little Book of Bedtime
The Little Book of Santa Claus

Printed in Great Britain
by Amazon